MAKING A LAW

A TRUE BOOK®

by

Sarah De Capua

Children's Press®
A Division of Scholastic Inc.

New York Toronto London Auckland Sydney
Mexico City New Delhi Hong Kong
Danbury, Connecticut

Hawaii state senators voting on a bill

Reading Consultant
Jeanne Clidas, Ph.D.
National Reading Consultant
and Professor of Reading,
SUNY Brockport

Content Consultant
Jonathan Riehl, J.D.
Graduate Instructor,
Communication Studies,
University of North Carolina,
Chapel Hill

The photo on the cover shows
a governor (at left) celebrating
with state legislators after
signing a bill into law.
The photo on the title page
shows the U.S. Capitol in
Washington, D.C.

Library of Congress Cataloging-in-Publication Data

De Capua, Sarah.
    Making a law / by Sarah De Capua.
        p. cm. — (A true book)
    Summary: Explains what laws are, how local, state, and federal laws are
made, and what citizens can do to participate in the lawmaking process.
    Includes bibliographical references and index.
    ISBN 0-516-22801-3 (lib. bdg.)   0-516-27941-6 (pbk.)
    1. Legislation—United States—Juvenile literature. 2. Statutes—
United States—Juvenile literature. 3. Legislation—United States—Citizen
participation—Juvenile literature. [1. Legislation. 2. Law.] I. Title. II. Series.
KF4945.Z9D4 2004
328.73'077—dc22   2003012507

CHILDREN'S PRESS, and A TRUE BOOK™, and associated logos are
trademarks and or registered trademarks of Scholastic Library Publishing.
SCHOLASTIC and associated logos are trademarks and or registered
trademarks of Scholastic Inc.
11 12 13 R 17 16 15 14

Contents

A person who drives faster than the speed limit is breaking the law and may be stopped by the police.

What Is a Law?

At some time you have probably heard an adult say, "There ought to be a law against that!" People who are frustrated with something often want a law passed to change it. A law is a rule made by the government that must be obeyed. A person who does not obey a law can face serious punishment. The punishment might be a **fine** or a jail term.

Starting with the **U.S. Constitution** and the Bill of Rights, Americans have passed thousands of laws. Most laws

Many states have laws against littering.

Don't Mess With Texas $10-1000 FINE FOR LITTERING

The U.S. Constitution was the first set of federal laws passed in the United States.

are created to protect people. Laws are also passed to provide services, such as public schools, public transportation, and programs to help people who are poor, elderly, or disabled.

Laws influence you every day. When you wear a seat belt while riding in a car, you are obeying a law. You also follow the law when you wait at a crosswalk for the sign to flash "walk."

Both of these laws were passed to keep you from getting hurt. Your seat belt will help pro-tect you in the car if there is an accident. Waiting at a crosswalk for the right time to walk out into the street protects you from

In most states, people are required by law to wear seat belts while riding in a car.

being hit by a car. Can you think of other laws you follow each day?

There are three different kinds of laws: local, state, and federal. Local laws are laws that people

In many areas, local or state laws require people to wear helmets while riding bikes.

in a certain community follow. State laws are followed by everyone in the state in which the laws are passed. Federal laws must be obeyed by everyone in the nation.

Making Local Laws

Usually, it's easier for people to have a direct effect on their local laws than on state or federal laws. Local governments pass local laws. In very small towns, meetings are held to make laws. Adults older than eighteen gather to discuss issues. These issues include

People voting at a town
meeting in a small community

what new laws should be
passed and how old laws should
be **enforced**. In town meetings,
every adult has a direct voice in
the local government. When
most of the people agree on an
issue, a law is passed.

Larger towns and cities have governments that are set up like state governments and the federal government. These governments have three branches: executive, legislative, and judicial. Each branch exists to keep

In large communities, a city council and a mayor work together to make local laws.

the others from becoming too powerful.

In local governments, the executive branch is usually headed by a mayor or supervisor. The legislative branch is usually a town or city council. The mayor and the council, all of whom are elected by the city's voters, work together to write and enforce local laws. In some communities, the council is called the board of aldermen or town board. The judicial branch includes the city's judges and their courts.

A mayor listening to the introduction of a bill during a city council meeting

PATRICIA C. BATES
MAYOR

Local governments usually address education laws, local taxes, health codes, and other local issues. Local governments cannot pass laws that go against state or federal laws.

A proposed law is called a bill. When a town or city council passes a bill, the mayor must approve and sign the bill before it can become a law. Mayors usually have veto power. To veto means to reject. If a mayor disagrees with and vetoes a bill, it will not become a law.

Some communities allow citizens to approve or reject laws through initiative or referendum. An initiative occurs when citizens collect enough signatures on a **petition** to put a proposed law

on a **ballot**. If enough people vote for the initiative, it becomes law. With a referendum, citizens vote to accept or reject a law that has been passed by the city or town council.

Making State Laws

New state laws usually begin as ideas for solving problems or improving life in a state. Many laws begin as citizens proposing solutions to problems. When many citizens in a community agree that a state law is needed, they take their idea to their state representative. Every state

Citizens asking their state lawmakers to reject legislation that would raise taxes

has a legislature, or lawmaking body. Most legislatures are divided into two houses: the state house of representatives (sometimes called the state

The Alabama House of Representatives in session

assembly) and the state senate. In some states, citizens also have the power of initiative and/or referendum.

When the state representative agrees with the citizens that a law is needed, he or she writes the idea into a bill and introduces it in the house. The bill is assigned a number, for example, HB 123. This stands for House Bill 123. Sometimes bills

An Arkansas state senator speaks to reporters about a bill she is sponsoring to raise the tax on tobacco products.

originate in the state senate. Those bills start with the letters "SB," for Senate Bill.

Public hearings usually follow the introduction of a bill. At these hearings, everyday citizens can tell their state leaders whether they think the bill is a good idea. After the hearings, the bill is discussed in a committee. If a bill passes in the committee, the committee believes it should be a law.

In many states, the bill next moves on to the full branch of

the legislature. If a bill is a house bill, it goes before the entire house of representatives for a vote. If it passes, the bill goes to a vote in the state senate. If a bill is a senate bill,

Georgia state representatives discussing a bill

it goes before the entire senate for a vote. If it passes, the bill is sent to the house of representatives for a vote.

Once a bill passes in both houses, it goes to the governor. The governor is the leader of a state. If the governor signs the bill, it becomes law. The governor can also veto the bill. However, if most of the state legislators vote to override the veto, the bill can become law

Members of the Tennessee House of Representatives vote on a bill increasing the state sales tax.

After signing a bill, a governor shakes the hand of the state representative who sponsored the bill.

even without the governor's signature.

How long do you think it takes to pass a state law? In some cases, it takes many years to complete all the steps to turn an idea into a law.

Silly State Laws

Most laws are passed to ensure personal and public safety. Some laws, however, are so silly that it's hard to understand why they exist. Here are some actual state laws. Do you think they are enforced?

Connecticut: In order for a pickle to officially be considered a pickle, it must bounce.

Georgia: No one may carry an ice cream cone in his or her back pocket on Sundays.

Indiana: It is illegal to take a bath between the months of October and March.

Minnesota: A person may not cross the state line with a duck on top of his or her head.

New York: Slippers are not to be worn after ten o'clock at night.

Pennsylvania: It is illegal to sing in the bathtub.

Making Federal Laws

Federal laws must be followed by everyone in the United States. The U.S. government is divided into three branches. The executive branch is made up of the president and his advisers. The judicial branch is made up of federal judges and their courts. The legislative

This photo shows members of the Senate and House of Representatives gathering to start a new session of Congress.

branch, called Congress, is made up of two houses: the House of Representatives and the Senate. The people of each state elect representatives and senators to serve them in Congress.

Congress is responsible for making national laws. Sometimes, the president suggests new laws.

A woman displays photos of drunk-driving victims in an effort get Congress to pass stricter laws against people who drive after drinking alcohol.

Lobbyists are politically active citizens who work to convince members of Congress to either support or reject bills.

Members of Congress have ideas for new laws too.

A law begins when a member of Congress decides to write a bill and introduce it in Congress. If the person serves in the House of Representatives, the bill is first presented to the House. It receives a name and number, such as HR 123.

If a member of Congress serves in the Senate, the bill is first presented to the Senate. It, too, receives a name and number, such as S 123.

The bill is placed before a committee for discussion. There are many different committees in each house of Congress. Each committee receives only the bills that are within its area of policy. For example, one

committee holds hearings on
bills related to foreign trade.
Another holds hearings on bills
related to public education. It
can take many months for a
committee to discuss a bill. If

the committee votes in favor of the bill, the bill is then voted on by the full house of Congress in which the bill began.

The House and the Senate each must pass the same version of a bill for it to become law. Usually, this means that a member of the House and a member of the Senate will work together, introducing identical bills at the same time.

However, members of Congress often want to make **amendments,** or changes, to

A board tallying the votes of U.S. representatives for or against a bill

bills. So even if members of the House and Senate cooperate, they may not pass identical bills. When this happens, a committee of senators and representatives must meet to agree on a **compromise** bill that everyone can support. This compromise version then goes back to the Senate and House for another vote.

Finally, after identical bills pass both houses of Congress, the bill is sent to the president. If the president signs the bill, it becomes a law. The president also has the power to veto a bill. Congress, however, can override the veto. To do this,

President George W. Bush signing a bill into law

two-thirds of those present in each house must vote to override the president's veto. If this happens, the bill becomes a law even without the president signing it.

You and the Law

The kinds of laws people live under and the ways they are enforced can make life in a certain place good or bad. Ordinary citizens in the United States can have a say in the kinds of laws that are made. They can contact their local, state, or federal leaders and

Citizens can demonstrate to send messages to their lawmakers.

tell them what they think about issues. Most leaders listen to the citizens they represent. They may decide which way to vote on a bill based on what the citizens say.

Do you think you're too young to have a voice in the kinds of laws that are passed? Don't be so sure! Kids your age can have a say too. In fact, in 1997, school-children in Washington State asked their state lawmakers to pass a law making the green darner dragonfly the state insect. They worked hard—and succeeded!

If there is an issue you care about, find out everything

In 1997, schoolchildren convinced their state legislators to pass a law making the green darner dragonfly the Washington state insect.

you can about it. Ask adults any questions you may have. Listen to other people's opinions. This will help you

You can contact your legislators to let them know what you think about important issues.

know all the facts. Get the name and address of the law-maker with whom you want to share your views. Write him or her a polite, respectful letter. What other ways can you think of to contact your government leader? Remember you are never too young to make a difference. Maybe you will see one of your ideas become a law!

President George W. Bush talks to students after signing a bill to improve child safety.

To Find Out More

Here are some additional resources to help you learn more about how and why laws are made:

 **Books**

De Capua, Sarah. **Paying Taxes.** Children's Press, 2002.

De Capua, Sarah. **Voting.** Children's Press, 2002.

Quiri, Patricia Ryon. **The Bill of Rights.** Children's Press, 1999.

Quiri, Patricia Ryon. **The Constitution.** Children's Press, 1999.

Organizations and Online Sites

**Congress for Kids—
Making Laws**
*http://www.congressforkids.
net/makinglaws.htm*

Find out how a bill
becomes a law and play a
related trivia game.

**Library of Congress—
How Laws Are Made**
*http://www.thomas.loc.gov/
home/lawsmade.toc.html*

Here you can find an expla-
nation of the lawmaking
process.

Making Laws that Last
*http://www.usdoj.gov/
kidspage/getinvolved*

You can show this class-
room activity to your
teacher. Your class can look
at the lawmaking process
and discuss what you think
makes a law good or bad.

Your State's Homepage
*http://www.state.(type your
state's two-letter ZIP code
abbreviation here).us*

If you type the above
address into your web
browser, substituting your
state's two-letter zipcode
(for example AL, AR, CT, IL,
ME, RI, WA, etc.) you'll find
your state's homepage.
Once you access it, you
can find all kinds of information about how your
state's government is run,
as well as information
about town and city
governments.

Important Words

amendments changes made to bills, laws, or legal documents

ballot secret way of voting, such as on a machine or on a slip of paper

compromise agreement that is reached after people with opposing views each give up some of their demands

enforced made sure that a law or rule is obeyed

fine sum of money paid as a punishment for doing something wrong

petition letter that is signed by many people and that tells those in power how the signers feel about a certain issue or situation

U.S. Constitution document containing the principles by which the United States is governed

Index

Meet the Author

Sarah De Capua works as an editor and author of children's books. As the author of many nonfiction works, she enjoys educating children through her books. Other titles she has written in the True Books series include *Becoming a Citizen, Being a Governor, How People Immigrate, Paying Taxes, Running for Public Office, Serving on a Jury,* and *Voting.*

Born and raised in Connecticut, Ms. De Capua currently resides in Colorado.